About me

T0342904

My birthday: _____ --

Where I live: _____

languages I know

Write the languages you know.
Tick (✓) the boxes.

Interesting!

Great!

Language: _____

I speak this language:

at home ☐   at school ☐   in the street ☐   on holidays ☐

Language: _____

I speak this language:

at home ☐   at school ☐   in the street ☐   on holidays ☐

Language: _____

I speak this language:

at home ☐   at school ☐   in the street ☐   on holidays ☐

Other languages: _____

_____

_____

My English language skills

1 What do you do in English? Complete the sentences.

Listening	I listen to _____English songs_____ . I listen to _____ .	☺
Reading	I read _____ _____ .	☺
Speaking	I speak to _____ _____ .	☺
Writing	I write _____ _____ .	☺

2 Do you like doing these things in English? Colour the faces.

Yellow = It's fantastic.

Blue = It's good.

Green = It's okay.

Red = It's difficult.

I can ...

Units 1-2

1 🎧 Listen and number.

2 💬 Say. Tell your friend about someone in the class. Don't say their name. Can they guess who it is?

> This person is tall. She's got long black hair ...

3 🔍 Read and match. Write the numbers.

1 Yes, I have.   2 No, I don't.   3 Yes, I can.

a Do you live in New York? 2

b Can you play the guitar? ☐

c Have you got a lot of brothers and sisters? ☐

d Do you like spiders? ☐

e Have you got a pet? ☐

f Can you play tennis? ☐

4 ✏️ Write about you.

What do you look like? What have you got?
What do you like? What can you do?

Tick (✓): I can do it!	
Easily	With help
1	
2	
3	
4	

I can ...   # Units 3-4

	Tick (✓): I can do it!	
	Easily	With help
1		
2		
3		
4		

1  Listen and say.

a  b  c  d

2 💬 Ask your friend the questions.

(Did you play a game yesterday?)

1 play / game / yesterday?
2 eat / fruit and vegetables / yesterday?
3 what / do / after dinner / last night?

3 🔍 Read about the school club. Answer the questions.

> ## Come to the school photography club!
>
> Have you got a camera? Do you like taking photos?
> Then this is the club for you. Pay £2.00.
> Bring your camera. We meet every Friday after school
> in the library, from 4.30 to 6.30.

a Where does the club meet? _____
b When does it meet? _____
c What do you have to bring? _____
d How much does it cost? _____

4 ✏️ Write about your club.

My club is _____

_____

4

I can ... Units 5-6

1 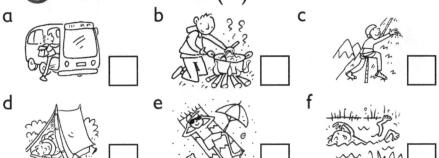 Listen and tick (✓). What did Sam do?

a b c

d e f

2 💬 Say. Compare two things.

> The cinema is better than watching TV because ...

cinema	TV
mountains	beach
a pet snake	a pet dog
travelling by plane	travelling by bus

3 🔍 Read and complete.

| clean   train   ~~world~~   paper   walk   off |

Help protect the 1 _world_ . Turn off the tap when
you 2 _____ your teeth. Catch a bus or a
3 _____ . Go to school on your bicycle.
Or you can 4 _____ ! Turn 5 _____ the lights
when you go out of a room. Put your glass,
6 _____ and cans in special bins.

4 ✏️ Write about your last English class.

What activities did you do? What did you learn?

_____

_____

Tick (✓): I can do it!		
	Easily	With help
1		
2		
3		
4		

I can ...   Units 7-8

Tick (✓): I can do it!		
	Easily	With help
1		
2		
3		
4		

1  Listen to the descriptions and say the names.

Jack   Laura   Kate

2 💬 Say. Tell your partner what you did yesterday. Use the words in the speech bubbles.

> In the morning I ...
> At school ... I ate ...
> I didn't ...

> In the afternoon I ...
> I played ... I walked ...
> I didn't ...

3 🔍 Read the recipe for a cheese and ham sandwich. Order the sentences.

- [ ] Cut the sandwich in half and eat it. Yum!
- [ ] Cut the cheese and ham.
- [ ] Put the top on the sandwich.
- [1] Put butter on the bread.
- [ ] Put the cheese and ham on the bread.

4 ✏️ Write a party invitation.

> ❀☙ Come to my party! ❧❀
>
> When _____
> Where _____
> Why _____
> Food and drink _____
> _____

Learning English

What do you like doing in English classes? Write 'yes',
'no' or 'sometimes' under the pictures.

Working in pairs and groups	Working alone	Using the book
Doing tests	Listening to the teacher	Listening to CDs
Practising pronunciation	Reading books	Doing projects
Doing arts and crafts	Acting	Speaking in groups and pairs
Singing songs	Playing games	Watching DVDs

7

My interests

Draw or stick a picture of something you like doing.

What's your hobby, sport or interest? _____

Where do you do it? _____

Why do you like it? _____

Who do you do it with? _____

_____

What do you need to do it? _____

_____

8

Our club

Draw a picture of your club.

What's your club called? --

Where do you meet? --

What time do you meet? --

What do you need to bring? --

What do you do there? --

A short story

Write and draw a story. It can be about something that happened to you or you can use your imagination.

You need an introduction (1), a middle (2 and 3) and an ending (4).

Title: _____

By _____

1 _____	**2** _____
3 _____	**4** _____

What's the best invention?

Draw or stick a picture of your favourite invention.

I like this invention because _____

It's better than _____ because _____

_____

With this invention you can _____

but you can't _____

I have this invention: **yes** / **no**.

A place I like

Draw or stick a picture of your favourite place.

Is it inside or outside? Is it a room in your home? Is it the cinema or a park? Is it the beach or the mountains?

Where is it? _____

When did you last go there? _____

What did you do there the last time you went? _____

_____

_____

_____

_____

A special event

Write about something special you did.

Was it a celebration (a street party, a birthday party or a wedding)?
Was it a day out (a picnic, a walk in the country, a shopping trip or a day at the zoo)?
Did you go out at night (to a concert, the cinema or the theatre)?

What was your special event? _____

Who went with you? _____

When did you go? _____

What did you do? _____

_____

Second Edition

Kid's Box 4
Language Portfolio

This Language Portfolio allows your pupils to build a record of their progress through the school year.

The content follows the units of **Kid's Box** and the structure corresponds to that outlined by the Council of Europe's European Language Portfolio.

Please visit our website to download the Language Portfolio teaching notes.

www.cambridge.org/kidsbox

CAMBRIDGE
UNIVERSITY PRESS
www.cambridge.org

ISBN 978-1-107-65461-7

9 781107 654617